796.62

CW01637434

Cycle Racing

WITHDRAWN

MACKWORTH TERTIARY COLLEGE
M0113627

Other cycling books available from Springfield Books:

Bicycle Mechanics: in workshop and competition
Steve Snowling and Ken Evans
160 pages • cased with jacket • ISBN 0 947655 14 X
A practical guide to maintaining your own racing bike.

Bicycle Road Racing: complete programme for training and competition
Eddie Borysewicz
276 pages • paperback • ISBN 0 941950 07 7

Cycle Racing
Ken Evans and Frank Westell
144 pages • cased with jacket • ISBN 0 947655 01 8
Covers all the main disciplines, and aims to turn riders into top-class performers.

Cycle Repair: step by step
Rob van der Plas
112 pages • paperback • ISBN 0 947655 44 1
Detailed instructional photographs throughout.

Cyclo-cross
Simon Burney
144 pages (approx) • cased with jacket • ISBN 0 947655 46 8
Available spring 1990.

Inside the Cyclist
Ed Burke
160 pages • paperback • ISBN 0 941950 06 9
A collection of articles on cycling physiology first published in *Velo-News*, America's leading cycle-racing journal.

Road Racing: technique and training
Bernard Hinault and Claude Genzling
208 pages • paperback • ISBN 0 947655 41 7
The training methods of a top European professional, five-times Tour de France winner Bernard Hinault.

Solo Cycling: how to train and race bicycle time trials
Fred Matheny
208 pages • paperback • ISBN 0 941950 10 7
The only comprehensive book on time-trialling in the English language.

The Complete Book of All-Terrain Bicycles
Eugene A Sloane
286 pages • paperback • ISBN 0 671 53233 2

The Complete Book of Long-Distance and Competitive Cycling
Tom Doughty
380 pages • paperback • ISBN 0 671 42434 3
Factual and comprehensive.

Take up Cycle Racing

Principal contributor:

Jim Hendry

Chief Executive
and former Director of Coaching Development
British Cycling Federation

SPRINGFIELD BOOKS LIMITED

Copyright © Springfield Books Limited and White Line Press 1989

ISBN 0 947655 57 3

First published 1989 by
Springfield Books Limited
Springfield House, Norman Road, Denby Dale, Huddersfield HD8 8TH

Edited, designed and produced by
White Line Press
60 Bradford Road, Stanningley, Leeds LS28 6EF

Editors: Noel Whittall and Philip Gardner
Design: Krystyna Hewitt
Diagrams: Steve Beaumont

Printed and bound in Great Britain

This book is copyright under the Berne Convention. All rights are reserved. Apart from any fair dealing for the purposes of private study, research, criticism or review, as permitted under the Copyright Act, 1956, no part of this publication may be reproduced, stored in a retrieval system, or transmitted in any form or by any means, electronic, electrical, chemical, mechanical, optical, photocopying, recording or otherwise, without the prior written permission of the copyright owner. Enquiries should be addressed to the Publishers.

Photographic credits
Cover photograph: Action-Plus
Tacx Wassenaar, Holland: 37
Graham Watson: 6, 12, 18, 20, 22, 23, 24, 25, 26, 27, 28, 39, 40, 41, 42, 45, 47
Noel Whittall: 15, 21, 44, 46

DERBY TERTIARY COLLEGE, MACKWORTH LIBRARY
DATE 17-4-91
ACC. NO. N60663
M011362

Contents

Introduction

The sport of cycle racing is more than a hundred years old, and during that time many different types of event have developed. These can range from sprints of a few hundred metres to road races which cover half a continent. There are off-road races which take you over the roughest country and there are indoor races on ballroom-smooth board surfaces. Somewhere in

this range there will be events which appeal to you, and by competing you will soon become fitter, stronger and get more fun out of life. Because the range is so large, this book deals mainly with events for road bikes and their close relatives which have developed for hard-track use, although cyclo-cross is also covered briefly, because it is such a popular winter activity for many types of racing enthusiast.

Although there are many different clubs and associations within the sport of cycling in Great Britain, the body which represents almost all of them and which controls cycle racing throughout the UK, is the British Cycling Federation (BCF). This book has been prepared with the assistance of the BCF. Readers who live elsewhere in the world should find out what their own national governing body is called. Details are available from the international organisations listed on page 48.

Cycle racing is not confined to any one age-group or sex; there are races for juveniles (under 16) and juniors (under 18) right up to veterans (over 40). Veteran competitions are one of the fastest-growing sections of the sport.

Much of your cycling activity will be on public roads. Road safety and good road manners are essential at all times, whether you are racing, training or just riding to the shops.

How do I get started?

Well, don't rush straight out and buy a bike just yet. If you do not already own one, take a good look at all aspects of the sport and decide which one appeals to you most. Make sure that what you want to do is possible – there's no point in setting your mind on track racing if there's not a velodrome within easy reach!

Your local cycling club is the best starting-off point, but again, don't rush. There may be three or four in your area, each of which specialises in different types of competition. Some may be touring clubs with no racing section at all, which is fine if social touring is your aim, but not ideal if you really have competition in mind, so check them out before you join. Try to pick one which has regular training runs as well as races. If possible, go for one with a coach who will devote time to your age-group.

Once you have made contact with a club, you will get plenty of advice – often more than you can handle at one time! However, you will soon find out which dealers in lightweight bikes the members trust, and should then be able to avoid buying an unsuitable machine.

1

Getting the bike right

A bike is a highly technical piece of equipment, and has to be carefully chosen to suit you. A glossary of the terms you will encounter appears on page 43. Take some time and trouble to make sure that you end up with the right machine – a bike which isn't the correct size is as bad as a pair of tight shoes. We'll assume that you are looking for a machine which you can use for regular riding on the road as well as for your first racing season. On this bike you will be able to get fit and develop the riding style which will suit *you* best. Let's take a look at the main components:

The frame

The frame is the heart of the bike. If you don't get this right, you will never be really comfortable or efficient on your machine. Measure your inside leg from crotch to ground (no shoes on), and use the table to find the size you will need. A good dealer will not let you choose an incorrect size, but if you are buying on the secondhand market you must be careful.

Table 1: frame sizes

Inside leg	Seat tube	Top tube
29.0	19.0	19.0
30.0	20.0	20.0
31.0	21.0	20.5
32.0	22.0	21.0
33.0	23.0	22.0
34.0	23.5	22.5
35.0	24.5	23.0
36.0	25.0	23.5
37.0	25.5	24.0
38.0	26.0	24.5

All measurements are in inches, and the inside leg is measured from the crotch to the ground.

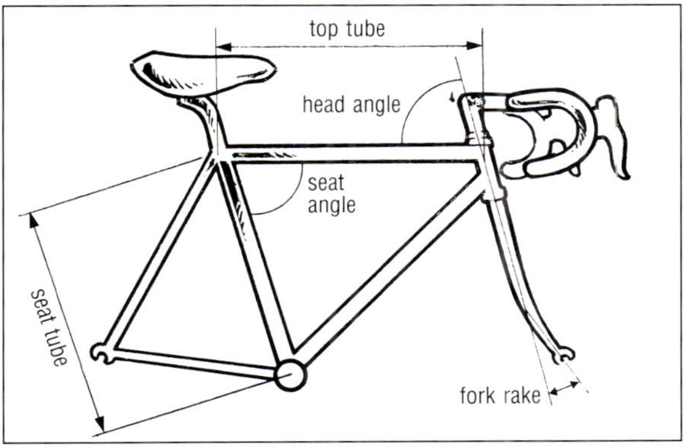

Fig. 1 The frame

You will often hear the *angles* of the frame mentioned: at this stage you do not need to worry too much about any of these except the head angle. This sets the angle of the front forks, and has a considerable effect on the handling of the bike. A steep angle (75°) will give rather "twitchy" handling and would be used on a track frame; 73° is a good choice for all-round fast roadwork.

The construction of the frame, and the materials it is built from, will depend to a large extent on how much you can afford to spend. As you will discover, lightness costs money! Spend as much as you reasonably can, and see that the money goes on good engineering rather than fancy paintwork. Stick to steel: at this stage you should avoid exotic materials such as carbon fibre even if you can afford them. You may see that frames are often advertised as being built from "double-butted" tubes; this means that the centre part of the tube has thinner walls than the ends. The result is a light tube which still has plenty of strength where it matters – at the joints with the rest of the frame.

The saddle

Plastic saddles have improved beyond all recognition, and are now produced with top-surface inserts such as suede leather. They are now popular in most branches of the sport, although some long-distance riders still prefer leather. If you do choose leather, remember that you will need to keep it as dry as possible at all times.

Positioning the saddle is easy if you follow these rules:

Set the *height* by putting one pedal in its lowest position; now, with your heel on the pedal, your knee

Fig. 2 Setting the saddle height

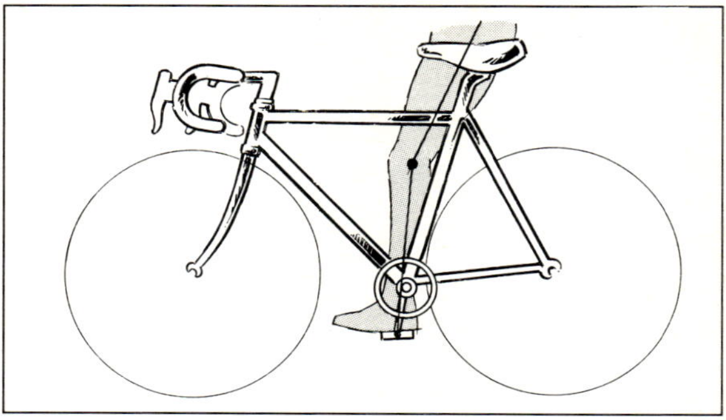

should still be *slightly* bent. Do this check without shoes on, and remember to raise the saddle a fraction more to allow for the thickness of the sole of your cycling shoes.

Set the *fore-and-aft* position as shown in Figure 3.

Fig. 3 When the crank is parallel to the ground, your knee joint should be directly above the pedal.

Handlebars and stem

Now that the saddle is correctly positioned, you can tackle the handlebars. These should be about the same width as your shoulders. You find out the stem length you will need by placing the back of your elbow against the point of the saddle. With your forearm horizontal, the centre of the handlebars should be about 3–5cm ahead of the tips of your fingers.

Wheels and tyres

Your bike should have 27in wheels, assuming you have a normal-size frame. The 26in wheel size is for

Fig. 4 Positioning the handlebars

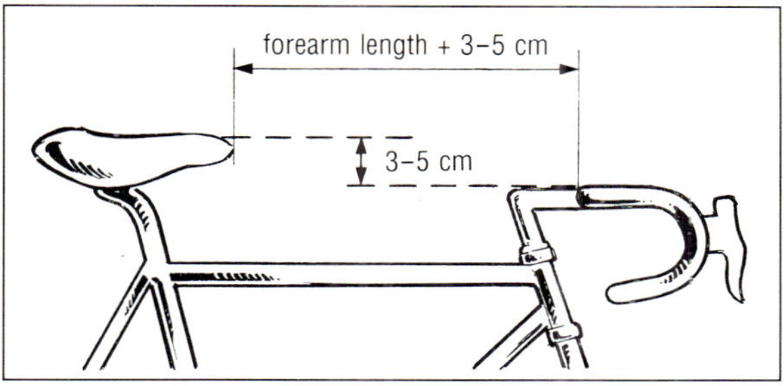

Fig. 5 Different types of rim and tyre

use with small frames only (under 19½in). As a newcomer to the sport, strength and reliability are more important than the ultimate in performance. Do not go for tubular tyres (*tubs*) yet – they involve more work and expense than you need to get involved with at this early stage. High-pressure tubed tyres, or the newer lightweight *700C* covers, are what you should be using. You will need alloy rims, but don't fall into the trap of going for lightness by getting the 28-spoke type. These are for track use, and won't stand up to the punishment they will get on ordinary roads. Stick to the normal 36-spoke arrangement, and make sure that they are tensioned so that the rim runs absolutely true.

As far as hubs are concerned, the sealed-bearing type will give the best service, but the older type with adjustable bearings are perfectly satisfactory if they are kept clean and lubricated regularly.

Brakes and transmission

Go for good quality, workman-like equipment rather than the latest gimmicks. High-grade maintenance and careful adjustment make all the difference. The brake shoes must *not* be allowed to rub on the rims at all when the brakes are off. Cable-runs must be smooth and lightly lubricated, and there must not be any frayed wires in the cables.

Riding styles vary — spend time making sure that the positions at the brake levers and handlebars really suit you. Note also that the rider above is wearing track mitts: these or gloves are essential safety protection when racing or training.

The position of the hooded brake levers can make a big difference to the feel of the bike; you will spend quite a lot of your pedalling time holding the hoods rather than gripping the handlebars themselves. Experiment with altering their position by a centimetre or so until your wrists feel completely comfortable.

The chainset, cranks, pedals and gears are vitally important, and the usual rule about quality before gimmicks cannot be stressed too highly. Crank length plays a big part in the way your power gets to the back wheel, so take some trouble to get this right. For a male of average physique, 167.5 or 170mm are the usual choices.

Competition cyclists need some method of keeping their feet in the right position on the pedals. Toe clips, used with plates fitted to the soles of cycling shoes, have long been the accepted way of doing this.

However, there is now a move towards a combination of special shoes and pedals which fit together securely. Currently the *Time* and *Shimano* systems are considered to represent the "state of the art". These are a great improvement on the older system, and do not come into the "worthless gimmick" category, although they can be rather expensive.

You can train using a cycle with only one gear, but realistically you should aim for a minimum of five, operated by a derailleur mechanism. This can easily be increased to ten gears if a double chainwheel is fitted.

The gearing of a cycle is usually still expressed in inches. Originally it was the diameter of the front wheel on an *ordinary* cycle (a penny-farthing bike). Obviously, the bigger the wheel, the further you travelled for each turn of the pedals. When the "safety cycle" (the modern bike) with its relatively small wheels and chain transmission came along, the gearing was still expressed as if it was driven by one huge wheel. Table 2 shows how different numbers of teeth on the chainwheel and rear sprocket affect the gearing. You will see that a big chainwheel and a small rear sprocket results in a high gear, and vice versa. There is absolutely no point in going to extremes of gearing. If you are going to use a single gear, it should be around 64–68 inches. You are aiming at developing an easy, supple pedalling style – not muscle-straining top speed at any cost!

Table 2: gear chart in inches (27-inch wheels)

	CHAINRING SIZE																	
SPROCKET SIZE	**36**	**38**	**40**	**41**	**42**	**43**	**44**	**45**	**46**	**47**	**48**	**49**	**50**	**51**	**52**	**53**	**54**	**55**
12	81.0	85.5	90.0	92.2	94.5	96.7	99.0	101.2	103.5	105.8	108.0	110.2	112.5	114.7	117.0	119.2	121.5	123.7
13	74.8	78.9	83.1	85.1	87.2	89.3	91.4	93.4	95.5	97.6	99.7	101.8	103.9	105.9	108.0	110.0	112.1	114.2
14	69.5	73.3	77.1	79.1	81.0	82.9	84.9	86.8	88.7	90.6	92.6	94.5	96.4	98.3	100.3	102.2	104.1	106.0
15	64.8	68.4	72.0	73.8	75.6	77.4	79.2	81.0	82.8	84.6	86.4	88.2	90.0	91.8	93.6	95.4	97.2	99.0
16	60.8	64.2	67.5	69.1	70.9	72.5	74.3	75.9	77.6	79.3	81.0	82.7	84.4	86.0	87.8	89.4	91.1	92.8
17	57.2	60.4	63.6	65.1	66.7	68.3	69.9	71.5	73.1	74.6	76.2	77.8	79.4	81.0	82.6	84.2	85.7	87.3
18	54.0	57.0	60.0	61.5	63.0	64.5	66.0	67.5	69.0	70.5	72.0	73.5	75.0	76.5	78.0	79.5	81.0	82.5
19	51.2	54.0	56.8	58.3	59.7	61.1	62.5	64.0	65.4	66.8	68.2	69.6	71.1	72.4	73.9	75.3	76.7	78.2
20	48.6	51.3	54.0	55.3	56.7	58.0	59.4	60.7	62.1	63.4	64.8	66.2	67.5	68.8	70.2	71.5	72.9	74.2
21	46.3	48.9	51.4	52.7	54.0	55.3	56.6	57.8	59.2	60.4	61.7	63.0	64.3	65.5	66.9	68.2	69.4	70.7
22	44.2	46.6	49.1	50.3	51.5	52.7	54.0	55.2	56.5	57.6	58.9	60.1	61.4	62.6	63.8	65.0	66.2	67.5
23	42.3	44.6	47.0	48.1	49.3	50.4	51.6	52.8	54.0	55.2	56.3	57.5	58.7	59.8	61.0	62.2	63.4	64.5
24	40.5	42.7	45.0	46.1	47.3	48.3	49.5	50.6	51.8	52.9	54.0	55.1	56.3	57.3	58.5	59.6	60.7	61.8
25	38.9	41.1	43.2	44.3	45.4	46.4	47.5	48.6	49.7	50.8	51.8	52.9	54.0	55.1	56.2	57.2	58.3	59.4
26	37.4	39.5	41.5	42.6	43.6	44.6	45.7	46.7	47.8	48.8	49.9	50.9	51.9	53.0	54.0	55.0	56.1	57.2
27	36.0	38.0	40.0	41.0	42.0	43.0	44.0	45.0	46.0	47.0	48.0	49.0	50.0	51.0	52.0	53.0	54.0	55.0
28	34.8	36.6	38.6	39.5	40.5	41.4	42.4	43.4	44.4	45.3	46.3	47.2	48.2	49.2	50.1	51.1	52.0	53.0
29	33.5	35.4	37.2	38.1	39.1	40.0	41.0	41.9	42.8	43.7	44.7	45.6	46.5	47.5	48.4	49.4	50.3	51.2
30	32.4	34.2	36.0	36.9	37.8	38.7	39.6	40.5	41.4	42.2	43.2	44.1	45.0	45.9	46.8	47.7	48.6	49.5
31	31.3	33.1	34.8	35.7	36.6	37.4	38.4	39.2	40.1	40.9	41.8	42.7	43.6	44.4	45.3	46.2	47.0	47.9

Accessories

Items such as pumps and water bottles are a matter of personal choice, but do pay particular attention to the way they are fitted to the bike. They must be properly secured, otherwise they will be a danger to yourself and others.

Good lights are vital if you are going to be riding after dark. Your budget must include enough to replace the batteries as a matter of routine the minute the lights show any sign of dimming. In the UK, the rear lamp must be to British Standard BS 3648, and you must also carry a reflector marked BS AU40 LT, which may be incorporated into the lamp.

Many enthusiasts will suffer unnecessarily to avoid having mudguards on their machine, but if you are planning to go training in all weathers, don't dismiss them. If the design of your frame allows mudguards to be fitted, it is well worth the marginal effect they have on performance to avoid getting salty road dirt sprayed all over yourself and your bike.

The secondhand bargain

By all means buy a secondhand bike – most of us started that way – but do be careful. Take someone with you who has good knowledge and judgement, and beware of being carried away by your own enthusiasm. It is all too easy to be attracted to a particular bike because it carries the name of one of your heroes, or maybe has a special feature you have always admired. Unless the frame is the right size and it is all in good condition, *don't buy it!*

At the same time that you buy your bike, spend a little more on a few spanners and keys which will fit it properly. There is a terrible temptation to "make do" with tools which have been in the family for generations, and these will often do more harm than good. Check whether your bike will need metric Allen keys – most do these days – and invest in a set. The cost will be insignificant compared with the value of the machine, and will repay itself many times over.

If you have followed the advice given in this chapter, you will have a bike which fits you, works smoothly and is safe. It may not be the ultimate racing machine, but on it you will be able to get fit and learn the craft of sport cycling. As your career develops you will gradually acquire more specialised equipment to suit the events in which you take part.

A racing bike of the 1880s. The front-wheel size of the old "penny-farthing" bicycle of the last century still affects the way we measure the gearing of today's machines.

Thermal clothing is a must for winter training – even on the sunny days.

2

What to wear

There is a great selection of cycle clothing on the market, and you should be able to find the right gear for any conditions. The airflow which keeps you cool in summer by evaporating your perspiration away, can very soon chill you in winter; you need to get your choice right.

Year-round essentials

Cycling comfort starts right where your body meets the saddle, and the rule here is always to wear proper cycle racing shorts with a chamois seat insert next to your skin – forget about Y-fronts for cycling. Correctly fitting racing shorts mean that you will not suffer from chafing from the seams of ordinary underwear. You will have to be very careful to keep your shorts absolutely clean by washing them after each race or training session. Use soap for this, not detergents, and dry the garment slowly to keep the chamois soft and supple.

Once you have got used to the idea that racing shorts are a must, there is great freedom of choice for the rest of your outfit.

Look after your hands and feet. Never ride without gloves or track mitts and well-fitting cycling shoes. Gloves are not just for warmth – they also provide essential protection in case your hands come into contact with the tarmac.

The shoes are an unavoidable expense, and ideally you will have a pair of relatively heavy-duty ones for winter, and lightweight perforated ones for summer racing.

Your head needs covering too. A woollen ski cap is a popular choice for cold weather, or a cotton cap if it is warmer. Special cyclists' versions of each are readily obtainable.

For racing you will need a helmet – the usual choice is the familiar padded leather cycling helmet which has stood the test of time. It is quite common to use this for training too.

Lightweight hard-shelled crash helmets are preferred by some riders and disliked by others. Their use is very much a matter for personal choice. If you decide that one is for you, be very critical when buying it: try on several different types, and choose the most comfortable. Ventilation holes are a must, and take care that the straps will not cut against your ears. Also, reject any hat which tends to work forward over your eyes if you nod your head vigorously!

One small item we can't recommend too highly is the addition of "Scotchlite"-type reflective patches on the heels of your shoes or the back of your calves if you are riding on the roads after dark.

Winter

If you live in a country where the winters are cold, it is vital to keep warm while training. The usual sporting rule applies of wearing many layers of thin garments rather than a few thick ones. A woollen undervest and long-johns are a good starting point for winter training, with a tracksuit top and pantalons as an outer layer. Extra warmth can come from adding a racing vest or a T-shirt or two under the tracksuit. The overall effect should be of clothes which are not so loose that they flap in the wind, yet not so tight that your circulation or movement is restricted. This is a good reason to use clip-on braces rather than a belt.

If you can afford one of the continental-style thermal training suits, fine, but don't be put off by having to make do with more ordinary garments.

Summer

So far we have stressed keeping warm, because it is usual to prepare your body for racing by training in the winter. When the season starts in spring, the racing cyclist can appear in a splendid selection of specialist clothing. According to the length of event in which you are entered, you can choose from "Lycra" skin suits and triathlon suits as well as more traditional racing vests and jerseys. Leg and arm warmers can be added as required on cooler days.

When the sun does shine, you must take precautions against sunburn. Cyclists are in particular danger here, because the cooling effect of movement through the air can mask the fact that your head and arms are soaking up excessive ultra-violet radiation. A cotton cap, and high-factor suncream on the face and arms, are sensible precautions.

3

Races and courses

The racing glossary on page 44 explains the expressions used to describe the many different types of race or competition. Here we look at the three main divisions: *road*, *time trial* and *track*.

Road racing

This is the form of cycle sport which is most commonly known to the public. Road racing covers the classic events such as the Tour de France and the Milk Race, as well as races over shorter closed circuits in city centres and public parks.

Road races are not always run over the smoothest roads...

The essence of this type of racing is that a large number of riders are close to each other for long periods of time. This has led to the development of a number of crafty techniques which enable a bunch of riders to cover the ground faster than they could as individuals. This is done by constantly changing the leaders of the bunch, so that no one spends more than a very short time exposed to the wind at the front. In theory, this ability of the bunch to travel more efficiently should lead to massed finishes as well as massed starts. Sometimes this is the case, and even after a couple of hundred miles the winner can be decided by a frantic sprint in the last few metres, but usually one or two small groups will manage to break away from the main bunch. Occasionally a lone rider will make an heroic break and attempt to string out a big gap many miles from the finish. All too often this sort of effort is unsuccessful and we see the lone rider's lead steadily broken down by the extra efficiency of the chasing group working temporarily as a team.

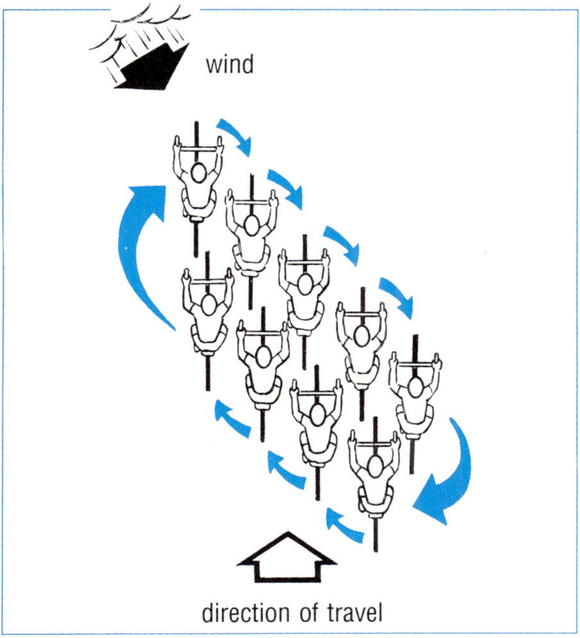

Fig. 6 How the riders "cheat" the wind: by taking turns at the front, then "resting" in the slipstream, a bunch can cover the ground faster than an individual. The formation will alter according to the wind direction, but the basic system of rotation within the bunch remains the same.

Road races are not always run over the smoothest roads...

Remember this if you find yourself in the middle of the field in one of your early races and are tempted to "go for it" alone. You may be amazed at how quickly you tire once you leave the protection of the bunch.

Although the classic style of road racing is the best-known type of racing, it is probably not the branch you will start in. Quite apart from the stamina required for the distances involved, you will need to have developed good bike-handling skills at racing speeds before getting involved with the cut-and-thrust of bunch racing.

Road time trialling

Quite often in the early hours of a summer Sunday morning you will see a lone racing cyclist hammering along an almost deserted stretch of main road. Then a moment later another rider appears in the distance, then another and another. These are time triallists, who set off at one-minute intervals. It sounds so simple: just ride along a main-road route of 10, 25, 50 or 100 miles as fast as you can. Yet this is one of the most challenging competitions in cycle sport.

Although the events take place on public roads, time trialling is a different sport from road racing. It is hard on the riders, but easier on the bikes, which can be lighter and slightly less rugged than road racers. Usually the course is a length of dual carriageway, with the start and finish on opposite sides, but quite close to each other. It will have been carefully measured, and chosen to avoid as many busy road junctions as possible. The halfway point will probably be a traffic roundabout, so that a non-stop ride is possible.

Naturally the winner is the competitor with the fastest time, but the riders are also competing against themselves. Each will be striving for a personal best. There is no opportunity for getting paced by another rider – in fact the rules forbid it. This is an event demanding personal strength and judgement, and also a knowledge of the weather conditions. The out-and-return nature of the courses is meant to cancel out the effect of wind, but it can still play a big part in your performance. You will need reserves of courage to keep going at maximum effort when a strong head-wind develops on the return leg.

BCF Time trial regulation no. 6:
Competitors must ride entirely alone and unassisted. They must not ride in company with, nor take shelter from, any other rider or from any other vehicle on the road. If one competitor overtakes another he must pass as widely as possible, and no shelter must be given or received. The onus of avoiding riding in company shall be on the rider overtaken who must drop back by at least 25 metres. Competitors when dismounted must wheel or carry their machines without assistance when covering any portion of the course.

Fixed-distance events are the most popular, because they are the easiest to organise; however, some trials are run for a fixed time such as twelve hours. These call for quite a large number of timekeepers to be placed around the course to record the positions of the riders when the time is up. The organisation required is considerable, and such events are rare.

Time trialling: a keen club rider at the half-distance turn point in a 25-mile event. Disc wheels were not permitted in amateur events until the 1989 season.

Team time trials are becoming increasingly popular. Teams of two, three or four riders work together, and it is the position of the last or sometimes next-to-last rider which decides the team's placing. Naturally, tactics are all-important in this event, with the lead constantly changing as riders take turns to "rest" in the slipstream of the others. The usual distance is between 40km and 100km, and the average speeds can be very high.

You can start to enter time trials on the type of bike we described in Chapter 1. As you gain experience, you may find that you want to specialise in this form of racing. You may also prefer a particular distance. That is the time to start thinking about the ultimate in lightweight equipment, and time triallers' bikes are tending to get more specialised each year. It is now quite common to see disc rear wheels and low-profile track-type frames which slope forwards being used by dedicated time triallers, but lack of such exotic machinery should not stop you from entering!

Olympic team time trialling – a pinnacle of the art.

Road time trial team on "low-rider" bikes.

Track racing

This covers the whole range of events on oval tracks. There is a variety of these, with lengths usually between 250 and 500 metres, although there are very steeply-banked indoor tracks which can be shorter than this, and flat grass ovals which may be longer. The races are always run anti-clockwise.

On the track, hundredths of a second are important, and the track bike is built with only efficiency in mind. The machine is reduced to the barest essentials; it has a single fixed gear, no brakes and no wing-nuts or quick-releases on the wheels. The saddle is very narrow, and the handlebars rather lower than on a road bike. Even more than in other forms of the sport, the bike needs to be exactly tailored to the rider; the gear ratio and crank length must match the sort of muscle power you can deliver. Track bikes, with the addition of a front brake, are occasionally used on the road, in time trials.

The latest track bikes – particularly those used for pursuit or track time trialling – have even lost the normal dropped handlebars and spoked wheels. The bars are short, upturned affairs, while the ultra-narrow wheels are built from carbon fibre or covered with a plastic membrane to cut the wind resistance caused by the spokes churning up the air.

Track events fall naturally into categories: *sprint*, *pursuit* and *time trial.*

Although from the name you would guess that the fastest of these would be the *sprint*, this is far from the case. Track sprinting is a sport of tactics, where the bikes may circle the track at a snail's pace before making a sudden violent burst of speed to the line. Each rider tries to remain high on the banking, just behind his or her rival, and at the best moment will jump into action and race past. The rear position is favoured because it allows both slipstreaming and a big element of surprise: the rear rider can pick the perfect position on the banking and can time the rush to start when the pedals are at the angle which allows maximum thrust. Before the first rider has realised that an attack has started, the second can be halfway to the line.

In *pursuit* racing, the riders start at opposite sides of the oval, and, as the name suggests, each tries to catch the other. This form of racing is a pure test of speed and stamina. At each half-lap, the riders can gauge whether they are gaining or losing ground by glancing across the track. It is quite rare for one to catch the other over the short distances of amateur pursuit races (4,000 metres maximum).

Left: *sprinters hammering for the line on traditional track bikes.*
Below: *from helmet to wheels, every detail of a dedicated track time trialler's equipment is designed to reduce drag.*

Team pursuit races are for teams of four, and tactics and team discipline are the key to success. Successful teams will have riders with well-matched abilities. The speeds can be high, and eight riders going absolutely flat-out around a tight indoor oval is a stirring sight.

Track time trials are for one rider at a time. The classic distance is one kilometre from a standing start. This is a much harder event than it looks, as it calls for extreme energy output for longer than is usual in a sprint. The choice of gear is difficult, too, because the choice must be made between a low one which helps rapid acceleration and a higher one which may allow a fractionally higher top speed to be held.

These three types of race are the ones you will most commonly see, but there are also a number of variations and specialities which you may become involved with once you have been in the sport for a little time. These include such delights as Madison and points races, and motor pacing. We have tried to cover most of these specialities briefly in the racing glossary which starts on page 44.

Successful track pursuit teams have to think together as well as ride together.

Cyclo-cross

Essentially a winter sport, cyclo-cross involves covering a cross-country course with your bike. It can involve riding on all types of terrain, running with the bike, and carrying it while you negotiate obstacles or up steep muddy slopes. It is an endurance sport which requires a high degree of overall fitness as well as specialised skills. The bikes used are closely related to road-going machines. They have to be light enough to be carried with ease, yet strong enough to stand the rough tracks.

Cyclo-cross was originally developed by road cyclists as a means of retaining competitive fitness during the winter months. Its appeal was such that riders began to specialise, and the sport gained World Championship status in 1950.

Cyclo-cross bikes must be strong, but light enough to carry easily.

The cyclo-cross season in the UK runs from early October to mid-February, and events are held throughout the country at weekends.The British Cyclo-cross Association (BCCA) holds National and Regional Championships for Seniors, Junior and Schools riders, and similar events are held in other countries. A recent development is to provide events catering for the *mountain bike* class of rider at cyclo-cross meetings.

You can gain good experience by entering cyclo-cross races just for fun, using an old "hack" bike. Many of the skills and much of the general training needed are similar to those for normal road racing.

The BCCA organises "come and try" events for beginners, and each cyclo-cross promotion starts with a special event for riders under the age of 12. These last between 10 and 15 minutes.

The trial days are great fun, and if you find that you have talents for cyclo-cross and want to become a serious competitor, you may well want to continue under the guidance of a BCCA coach, who will also give useful advice on buying a special cyclo-cross bike.

Whether you race off the road or on it, fitness is essential.

4

Fit to race

Cycle racing and training is strenuous exercise, and some care is essential: young people who are still growing should not take part in weight-training or significant overload-training as this may affect bone development and cause joint damage. Older riders who are taking up the sport after any length of time without physical exercise should have a medical check before starting.

Recreational cycling is wonderful exercise, but if you are entering into cycle sport, you should take things a stage further by starting a programme for race fitness. Here we suggest a winter training programme which will ensure that you will enjoy your first races when the season starts in the spring:

Preparation

Start a training diary. This may sometimes seem a bit of a bore, but very soon you will appreciate its value. You should record daily:

- heart rate on waking in the morning
- weight, taken at the same time each day
- details of training, both on and off the bike
- hours of sleep
- weather conditions when last out
- your assessment of your last race
- if you are still growing, you should also record your height monthly

Keeping a diary like this soon becomes automatic, and you can't start too soon. The BCF publishes an excellent purpose-made version.

Before any riding session which is going to be faster than gentle touring speed, you must carry out a stretching and warm-up routine. Here is a set of simple exercises which will keep you supple. Do them every day, regardless of whether you are going out on the bike.

1 Achilles tendon and calf stretch
Stand about a metre from the wall, with the palms of your hands against it. Keeping your feet flat on the ground, slowly bend your elbows until your forearms are flat against the wall. Feel this sorting out your calf muscles! Hold the position for one minute.

2 Twisting tone-up
Sit on the floor with your legs straight. Bend your right knee and put your right foot outside your left knee. Now twist from the waist as far to the right as possible and place your palms on the ground, *keeping your bottom firmly on the floor.* Try to relax your back, and hold the position for a count of ten. Easy. Now change legs and repeat the exercise in the other direction. Now do it all five or ten times...

3 Thoracic stretch
Sit upright, cross-legged on the ground. Raise both arms, with palms facing forward. Curve your back, flexing your chest, and return upright. Hold for five seconds, and flex again. Repeat five or ten times.

4 Shoulder stretch

Stand with legs apart and arms in front of you with fingers interlaced and your palms facing away from you. Now, keeping your chin tucked in, steadily raise your arms above your head as far as they will go. Hold for one minute. Swing your arms and shoulders a bit before going on to the next exercise.

5 The rocker

Lying on your stomach, reach back and grasp your ankles. Arch your back and pull hard, lifting your thighs off the floor so that you can rock on your lower abdomen. Hold for one minute. Partway through you may wonder if it is all worth it.

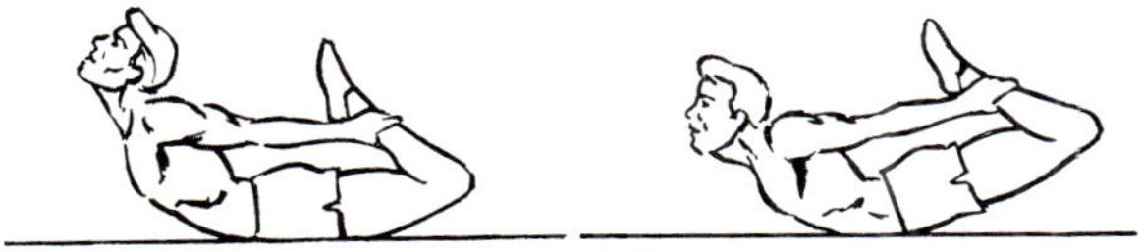

6 Hamstring stretch

Keeping your legs straight, place your right heel on a table about hip-high. Grasp the right leg with both hands as near the ankle as possible. Now bend your trunk and try to touch your leg with your head. When you reach the stretch-pain, ease off, then press again. Hold for one minute. Repeat four times for each leg.

7 Lateral stretch

Stand with your legs apart, and keep your back upright throughout the exercise: bend to the right, reaching as far down your leg as you can with your right arm and pressing your left fist into your left armpit. Hold for 30 seconds, then slowly repeat on the other side.

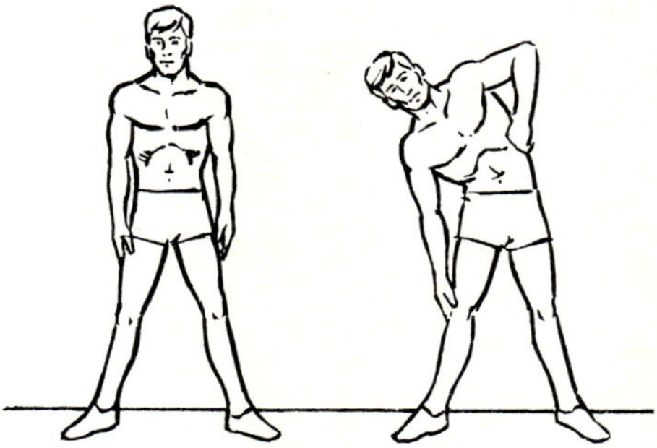

8 Abdominal stretch

Start by kneeling on hands and knees. Steadily move your bottom back to your heels and then extend your hands until your chest is on the floor. Hold for 30 seconds and repeat eight to fifteen times.

9 Quadriceps stretch

Lie on your side, and grasp your uppermost ankle. Gradually move your hips forward so that you can feel a good stretch in the thigh, and hold the position for a minute. Repeat four to eight times per leg.

10 Groin stretch

Sit on the floor with the soles of your feet touching. Push down on your knees as far as possible. Hold for one minute. Try to get your knees a little nearer the floor each day!

Food for performance

Now that you are well on the way to becoming a competitive cyclist, it will be worthwhile to give a little thought to what you eat. As your sport demands more energy, your appetite should automatically increase. All you need is to make sure that you eat a good *balance* of different foods and your body will do the rest.

You are aiming at the right mixture of *carbohydrates*, *fats* and *proteins*. The sort of carbohydrates which do most good are in food which has had little processing, such as wholemeal bread, fresh fruit and lightly cooked vegetables. Adequate fat is easily obtained by eating moderate amounts of meat, milk and cheese, so you should avoid excessively fatty foods such as chips. These foods all provide protein too, as do fish, eggs, nuts and green vegetables.

Remember, there's no single item which will make you stronger – you must have a mixture. You can help your body by giving it food which it can process easily. Go for the following when you have a choice:

- Liver or kidneys rather than steak or pork
- Boiled or baked potatoes rather than chips
- Fresh fruit rather than sweets or chocolate
- Grilled food rather than fried food
- Pasta rather than hamburger
- Fruit juices rather than alcohol

Do learn to enjoy different foods and have plenty of variety. If you do this you will not need vitamin supplements or fancy diets.

Drink enough! Sufficient liquid intake is vital for any athletic activity, and cycling is no exception. You will inevitably sweat a lot, and this must be replaced or dehydration will set in. Take small drinks at frequent intervals before, during and after any event. Water, or *very dilute* glucose drinks, are fine: don't fall into the trap of thinking "I'll make it more concentrated for a bit of extra energy". That is sure to do more harm than good because your digestive system will have to provide water to dilute the solution to a strength which is acceptable to your body. This will mostly have to come from your blood, disturbing the circulatory system, which is about the last thing you would want to happen in the middle of a training session or race.

5

Training

The first month

You should ease your body into training by going on plenty of steady rides. The pace should not be too hot – try for a steady pedalling rate of about 100 rpm. Avoid sudden bursts and "burn-ups" at this stage. You should aim to cover these weekly mileages:

12–15 years old:	100 miles
16–18	180 miles
18+	200 miles

Try to do 40 percent of your mileage on Sunday, 25 percent on Saturday, and fit in the rest as best you can during the week. These figures are only guidelines. Don't think that you *have* to cover the miles at all costs: if the weather is really bad, do some indoor training instead. If you are recovering from a cold or flu, *get better first*, then get back on your bike.

At the end of a training session, resist the temptation to stand around in your sweaty clothing getting chilled; the sooner you can have a bath or shower, the better.

Find the right training level

Once your body has become used to the idea of propelling a bike along at a moderate speed, you can start to increase the pressure a little.

Aerobic training

We will look at aerobic training first; this concentrates on developing your heart/lung efficiency so that your muscles can be efficiently supplied with the oxygen they need to keep on working. To find the fine line where leisure riding ends and training begins, you need to check your "training threshold", which is generally accepted as being 70 percent of your maximum heart rate (MHR). You can get a good idea of what *your* MHR is in beats per minute by subtracting your age from the figure 220. So if you are 20 years old, your MHR will be about 200; 70 percent of this is 140, and you need to ride hard enough in training to sustain that rate.

You can check your heart rate yourself by feeling your pulse with a fingertip each side of your Adam's apple. Count the beats in 15 seconds, and multiply by four to get the minute rate. Please don't do this while you are actually pedalling along the road!

Fig. 7 Checking your pulse

Start by riding for about an hour at this rate, and steadily work up until you can sustain it for three hours. It's hard work, but you will now be getting *quality* into your miles, and the rewards will follow. Aerobic training is a sound base for any type of competition because it gets you fit enough to train for more specialised techniques.

Specialised training

Anaerobic training

Anaerobic training concentrates on developing the energy stored in your body which can be released without the use of oxygen. This is very intense, but lasts for only a short time. Anaerobic power comes into its own during sprints.

The best way to build the type of muscle fibres which deliver anaerobic power is by doing relatively short periods of work at 85 to 90 percent of MHR. Don't rush into this, particularly in the cold and wet days of winter – that is almost sure to lead to muscle and tendon strains. Training at this sort of load requires care, and beginners should be guided by a knowledgeable coach. In a club you will typically be introduced to high-intensity training during midweek sessions with a bunch of riders on a road course of four or five miles. At first you may only stay with the bunch for a lap or so, and be glad of the shelter a position at the rear provides. As your performance improves you will be with them for more laps, and will eventually be able to take ever-longer spells at the front.

Interval training

This is a strenuous form of stamina development training which is only suitable for riders who are at least 16 years old.

Interval training consists of performing repeated short bursts of intense activity in a controlled way. Road-race riders could try this programme:

- Select a flat stretch of road about 1½ miles long
- Ride for twenty minutes of steady warm-up
- Ride your chosen length as fast as possible: this is the base from which you establish your *target time*, which will be your *fastest time plus ten percent.* We'll assume your fastest time was 3 minutes, in which case your target time will be 3 minutes and 18 seconds.
- You now have to ride the course, repeating your target time as often as possible, with a three-minute rest between repetitions. If you go outside the target time for two repetitions, the quality has gone, and you should finish off with a steady 15-minute ride on low gears.
- The rest periods consist of steady pedalling in low gear.
- When you can produce 15 repetitions inside the target time, you must increase the workload by decreasing the rest period by 30 seconds, or by raising your speed by increasing the gearing. Only change one of these variables at any session, and never shorten the rest period below 1½ minutes.

This programme will build stamina; you can easily imagine how it will improve your ability to sprint to close gaps or to climb hills well – both great assets for a road rider.

You can improve leg strength for climbing by treating your bike as a weight-training machine. The technique is to pick a reasonable hill and then select a high gear which keeps your pedalling rate below 60 rpm. Remain in the saddle, and keep up the effort for periods varying from 30 seconds to two minutes, with short recovery periods in between. *This is a severe exercise which must not be used by juveniles or juniors.*

However, if you are going to concentrate mainly on track events, your interval training will need to be even more specifically tailored to your needs. Follow the BCF Training Manual if in doubt, and try to spend some time with a good coach rather than put a lot of effort into training that may not be appropriate. Although the key to a good start to the racing season is *quality miles* during the winter, there are many other things you can do to help get your body into racing form. A general fitness circuit-training programme which can be easily set up in your own home is well worthwhile, and your coach will advise on this. The "circuit" in this case is not a track, but a circuit of exercises such as sit-ups, press-ups and skipping which are performed in sequence. Circuit training is used by athletes of all types to prepare their bodies for specialised training.

The exercise bike

The ordinary home exercise bike is only suitable for retaining flexibility. For race training, you need a *windload simulator* type. These use the rear wheel of your own bike to drive a fan, and the resistance builds up much as it would if you were pedalling along a flat road. The benefits for winter training are obvious: no need to risk your health by breathing in icy-cold air, and no need to risk your neck by taking your chances with the traffic on dark, wet roads. Unfortunately boredom is a great deterrent to long periods on indoor trainers, and you will need strong self-discipline to keep at it. Sweat can also be a problem; because there is no breeze to carry it away, it tends to build up considerably. If you do use your bike on a windload simulator, be sure to protect it from the corrosive effects of sweat, and wipe it down carefully after every session.

Tacx windload simulator

6
Racing techniques and tactics

Before we begin to look at race-winning tactics, let's consider some race-losing ones:

- Poor preparation. Give your bike a really thorough check-over before the event as a matter of routine, and do a final check of all equipment immediately before the start.
- Poor starting. Practise getting your feet into the clips until you can do it without thinking about it, and without letting the bike wobble about. Learn not to rush doing up the toestraps – get properly settled on the bike first.
- Badly adjusted toestraps. There's just no excuse for track racers to "lose a pedal" at the start, yet it still happens, even at international level meetings.
- Unlaced shoes. Include these in your pre-race check. It is particularly important if you are using one of the new fixing systems which do not need toestraps.
- An empty water bottle. Don't wait until the race has started to discover that you forgot to fill it.

Group riding skills

You will have to get used to riding in a tight bunch, and not be intimidated by rubbing shoulders at speed. You will also have to develop the art of "holding a wheel" – tucking in behind another rider to take advantage of the shelter this offers, keeping no more than six or eight inches away for miles on end. The safe way to do this is to remain those few inches behind, and *slightly to one side*, so that if the other rider slows suddenly you can avoid your front wheel making contact. It is your front wheel which gets you into trouble – contact on your rear wheel rarely throws you off.

All the riders in this bunch are keeping just to one side of the bike in front, but they are concentrating on the road well ahead.

The best way to learn this type of tight riding is with your clubmates, practising 10- to 15-mile team time trials. One of the main tricks is to develop the knack of looking well ahead so that you can see obstacles or changes of direction coming up, while at the same time using your peripheral vision to sense your distance from the other bikes.

Track racing also teaches you bunch-riding skills, and even if you really want to specialise in road racing, you should include some track events in your experience.

Accidents are not entirely unknown...

Where in the bunch?

If you can, stay with the front quarter of the field. This is where the "sharp" riders will be, and crashes are less frequent than further back. You will also be well positioned to create attacks or answer them. You may feel that this is a little ambitious to start with, and be tempted to tuck in at the rear to see how things go. Forget it! Think positive and race positively from the start. You may find that the class is too good for you, and have to drop back, but at least you will have done the best you can. In fact, if you have trained well during the pre-season, you will probably place higher than you may have expected.

There are positive disadvantages to being at the rear, particularly in races with a lot of corners. This is because of the "accordion effect" which the pack develops on leaving each corner. City-centre races give a particularly good example of this – watch how the back markers have to slow more for the corners than they would if the road ahead was clear, and then see how much work they have to do to get back in touch again. On a twisty circuit this can happen a couple of hundred times in the course of a race, and it is not hard to imagine how energy-sapping that can be.

Cornering

Races can be won through good cornering technique. Your aim must be for total smoothness, with all the braking completed before you lay the bike into the bend, and the power on again at the earliest possible opportunity. You should be looking at the exit as you enter the corner, not down at the kerb: if you have to adjust your line halfway through, you have misread the bend and it is certain that you can save a few valuable hundredths of a second next time round.

If the corner is so tight that you have to freewheel, help your stability by transferring your weight onto the outside pedal. On twisting descents it is important to get the rhythm of weight transfer right.

Climbing

Climbing skills can play an important part in racing success. The most effective technique is to keep your hands on the "tops", pulling up on the bars and keeping your pedalling as rhythmic as possible. When you have to come out of the saddle, transfer your grip to the brake hoods and rock the bike from side to side, so that each downward stroke of the pedal has your full body-weight behind it – a technique popularly known among cyclists as "honking". Practise this so that you can do it effectively without letting the bike weave all over the road.

Sprinting

Most road races end in a sprint between a few riders, and sometimes between the whole bunch, so this is an important skill to develop. No doubt you will have tried some short sprints during club training runs. Make the most of this training so that on the day you can go for the line with confidence. You should remain "on a wheel" for as long as possible, saving your strength and trying all the time to assess the gradient, wind strength and direction and the distance to the line. Get into a gear that you will be comfortable with before pulling out to make your bid. Don't let the fact that you may be at the back of the field stop you from making a sprint for the line. You are a racer: every place is worth having, and every race is a practice for the next one. If you start by winning sprints for twentieth place, you will gain the experience needed to win that elusive first place one day.

Every place counts! Don't give up in the final sprint until you are over the line.

7

Glossaries

Cycling offers such variety that it is impossible to cover in depth all the technicalities or all the different branches of the sport. However, the following glossaries will explain some of the special expressions you will meet now that you have taken up cycling. Because France was the cradle of the bike, some of them are French words, and you may come across them pronounced in the French way, so we have given this pronunciation in square brackets where appropriate. French words are also marked with an asterisk (*).

Bicycle glossary

Allen bolt Bolt or screw with a six-sided recess in the head. Needs the right size of Allen key to undo it.

Block The set of sprockets on the rear hub.

Blocks The brake shoes.

Bottom bracket The bottom of the frame which carries the bearing for the pedal spindle.

Butted Where tubes or rods of different thickness are joined together to combine strength with lightness, eg *butted spokes*.

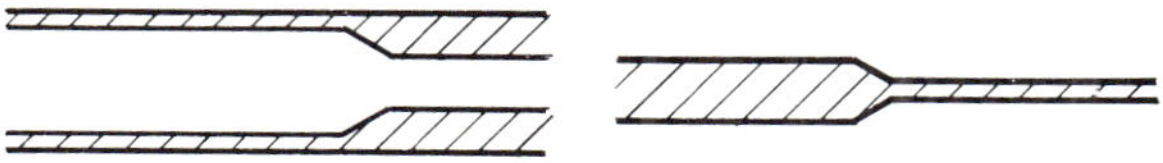

Fig. 8 Butted tube (left) and butted spoke (right)

Chainstays The frame tubes which run from the bottom bracket to the rear *dropouts*.

Chainset The *chainwheel* and crank assembly.

Chainwheel The large sprocket attached to the chainset cranks.

Cotter pin Slightly tapered pin which was used to hold the crank to the chainwheel spindle. Now obsolete on lightweight cycles.

Derailleur* Gear-changing mechanism which moves the chain from one *sprocket* on the *block* to another.

Drops Dropped handlebars. The normal type for sporting use. Riding "on the drops" means gripping the lower part.

Dropouts The slots in the forks into which the wheel spindles fit.

Granny gear Ultra-low bottom gear used on *mountain bikes*.

Hoods The part of the brake lever which is clipped to the bars.

Index Gear-change system which allows the gears to be found at a positively located position of the lever, rather than by "feel". Popular for *cyclo-cross* and *mountain bikes*.

Sprockets The gear-like wheels on the rear hub, around which the chain goes.

Tops The top of the handlebars, as opposed to the *drops*.

Tubs Very thin *tubular tyres*, made with a rubberised silk or cotton carcase to which a thin rubber tread is bonded. Stuck onto the rims with tyre cement.

Racing and event glossary

ATB (*All-terrain bicycle*) See *mountain bikes*.

BMX (*Bicycle Moto Cross*) A Californian import; provides exciting off-road racing for five-year-olds upwards. Highly organised.

Bonk Nothing to do with sex. The expression has long been used by cyclists to describe the condition of fevered fatigue brought on by riding too hard without suitable food intake.

Brevet* [brevay] See *Randonnée*

Cadence The rate of turning the pedals: eg 70 rpm.

Category Senior male members of the BCF are given licences to race in different categories, according to their skill and experience. If you are over 18, you will start in the Third Category, and move up to Second or First by gaining category points in qualifying events.

Criterium Road races held over several laps of a relatively short circuit of about eight miles. The maximum distance is 62 miles (100km), and time handicaps are often given.

Cycle speedway Racing on very short tracks (about 100 metres) for simple but specialised machines. Organised into leagues by the Cycle Speedway Council. Winter meetings are now often run indoors in sports halls.

Cyclo-cross A winter sport involving both riding and carrying the bike over very demanding off-road going.

Derny* Type of moped used for *motor pacing*.

Devil-take-the-hindmost Track race for a large number of riders over many laps. Last across the line on each lap drops out. Ends with a frantic sprint between the last three.

Madison Two-man team races where the first across the line scores. Originated at the six-day races at Madison Square Gardens.

Motor pacing Track racing behind a motorcycle or moped. Wind resistance is greatly reduced, and so speeds are high. Calls for great skill and judgement by both pacer and rider.

Mountain biking has become an important part of cycle sport within a few years. As well as competing among themselves, MTBs now often have a special class at established cyclo-cross events.

Mountain bikes (*ATB, MTB*) Another Californian import. Essentially small-framed bikes with large-section tyres and hordes of gears, built with cross-country performance in mind. Special races for these machines are becoming popular.

Omnium An event consisting of several (usually four) individual types of race: eg sprint, 1km time trial, pursuit, 5km points race.

Peleton* (or *peloton*) The main bunch of riders.

Points Points race; points are awarded to the leader each lap, with a big bonus for the final lap.

Prime* [*preem*] A special prize awarded to the first rider at a certain point during the course of a race. Can be on the flat, or, quite commonly, at the top of a hill.

Randonnée* [*rondonay*] A long-distance course (eg Lands End to John o'Groats) which has to be covered in a certain time. For people who like touring with a target, rather than outright racing. Progress is recorded on a card called a *brevet*, and randonnées are often called *brevet runs*. Organised in Great Britain by *Audax UK*.

Stage race A long-distance road race, such as the Tour de France, which is divided into daily stages. Can be held over a period of between 2 and 23 days.

Velodrome Banked circuit for track racing. May be outdoors or under cover.

Useful addresses

Great Britain

Audax United Kingdom Mr P J Aldridge, Jesmond, Farmhill, Stroud, Gloucestershire GL5 4BZ

British BMX Association Mr R W Peter, BBMXA, Beverley Buildings, 61 Bryn Street, Ashton in Makerfield, Wigan WN4 9AX

British Cycling Federation 36 Rockingham Road, Kettering, Northamptonshire NN16 8HG

British Cyclo-cross Association Mrs Joan Edwards, 59 Jordan Road, Sutton Coldfield, West Midlands, B75 5AE

Cycle Speedway Council Mr M Perkins, 9 Meadow Close, Hethersett, Norwich NR9 3DZ

Cyclists' Touring Club Cotterell House, 69 Meadrow, Godalming, Surrey GU7 7HS

English Schools Cycling Association Mrs L Crockett, 23 Welldon Crescent, Harrow, Middlesex HA3 6AB

UK BMX Association Mr J M Drew, 21 Sands Farm Drive, Burnham, Buckinghamshire SL7 1LD

Veterans Cycle Racing Association Mr C A Williamson, 24 Sunnybank Crescent, Greetland, Halifax HX4 8ND

Women's Cycle Racing Association Mrs M Swann, 41 Beccles Drive, Barking, Essex

International

Fédération Internationale Amateur de Cyclisme Via dei Campi Sportivi 48, 00197 Roma, Italy

Union Cycliste Internationale 6 rue Amat, CH-1202 Geneva, Switzerland